No, thank you!

By Janine Amos

Illustrated by Annabel Spenceley

CHERRYTREE BOOKS

A Cherrytree Book

Designed and produced
by A S Publishing

First published in 1998
by Cherrytree Books
a division of the Evans Publishing Group
2A Portman Mansions
Chiltern St
London W1U 6NR

Reprinted 2002 (twice), 2004

British Library Cataloguing in Publication Data

Amos, Janine
    No, thank you!. – (Good manners)
    1.Interpersonal relations – Juvenile literature
    I.Title II.Spenceley, Annabel
    395.1'22

ISBN 1 84234 123 5

Printed in Malaysia

Mum's cake

It is teatime. Mum has a cake.

Mum offers the cake to Owen.

The children forget to say thank you.
How does Mum feel?

Mum offers the cake to Rose.

9

Rose smiles and says No, thank you.

How does Mum feel now?

Too busy!

Nathan is drawing space rockets.

Josh comes up.

Nathan is busy.

How does Josh feel?

Josh goes over to Toby.

Toby is busy too.

How does Josh feel now?

Jenny and Clare

Jenny is building a palace.

It's wobbly!

Clare comes over.

25

How is Clare feeling?

Jenny thinks about it.

How does Clare feel now?

30

"We don't always want what people offer. And it's OK to say so kindly. If a friend offers you something you don't want or need, remember to say No, thank you with a smile."